Animal Antics

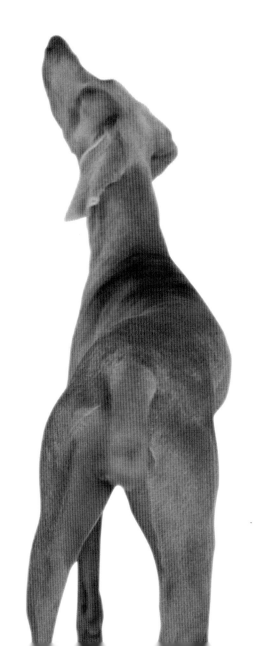

Animal Antics

A Dog Record Book

JUDY REINEN

haVoc
PUBLISHING INC.

Contents

Contents

My Arrival

I was born on

································

There were ··········

puppies in my litter

My Name

I am called ....

My Breed

I am a

....

We are known for

....

....

Photographs

Photographs

Best Features

My eyes are

My tail is

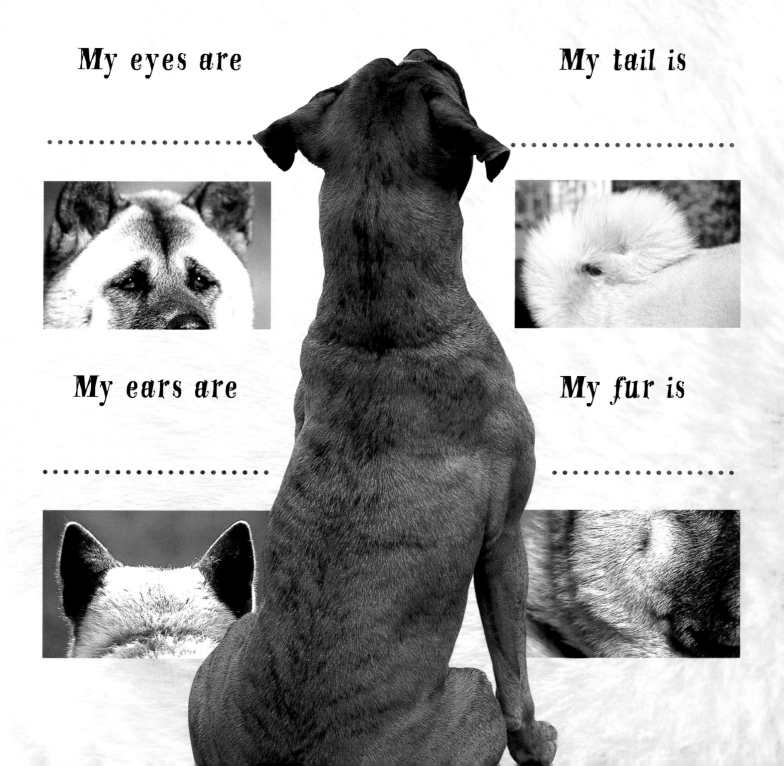

My ears are

My fur is

Lineage

Grandsire/Grandame

Grandsire/Grandame

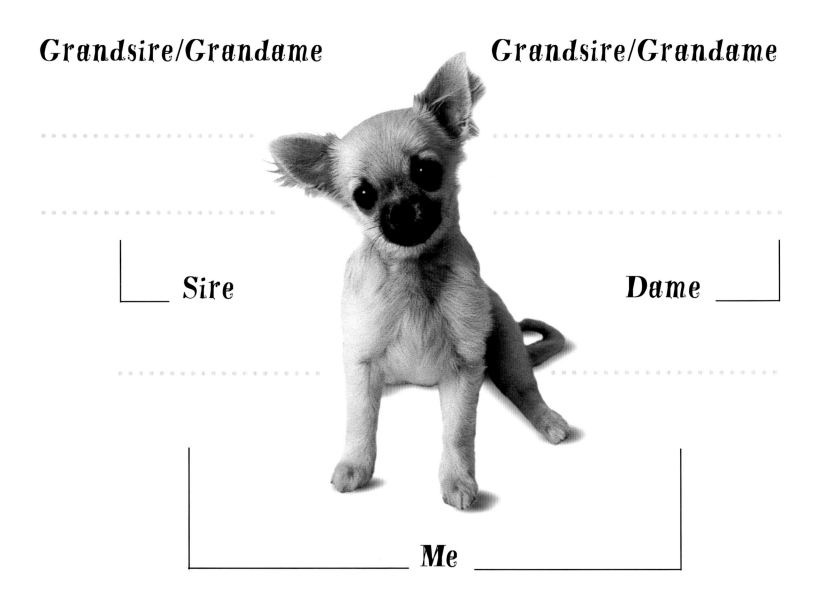

Sire

Dame

Me

My Family

My owner is ....

We live at ....

Family members ....

....

Other relatives ....

Photographs

Photographs

Growing Up

Special Moments

Birthdays

Year ....

For a present I got ....

Party guests ....

Year ....

For a present I got ....

Party guests ....

Birthdays

Year

For a present I got

Party guests

Birthdays

Year . . . .

For a present I got . . . .

Party guests . . . .

. . . .

. . . .

. . . .

Year . . . .

For a present I got . . . .

Party guests . . . .

. . . .

Photographs

Photographs

Christmas

Year ....

We spent the day at ....

For a present I got ....

Year ....

We spent the day at ....

For a present I got

....

Christmas

Year _____

We spent the day at _____

For a present I got _____

Christmas

Year ....

We spent the day at ....

For a present I got ....

....

Year ....

We spent the day at ....

For a present I got ....

....

Photographs

Photographs

Outings

Top spots

· ·

· ·

· ·

Special events

· ·

· ·

Outings

Top spots

Special events

Best Friends

My best friends are

· ·

· ·

Our favourite games are

· ·

· ·

Favourites

Favourites

Photographs

Photographs

Holidays

Holidays

Top Spots

Top Spots

Photographs

Photographs

Achievements

....

....

....

....

....

....

....

....

....

....

Exercise

My exercise routine

Grooming

Record

· ·

· ·

· ·

· ·

· ·

· ·

Bath Time

Flea Treatments

Date	Date	Date	Date	Date

Visits to the Vet

Date	Illness	Treatment

Worming & Vaccination

Worm Treatments

Date	Date	Date	Date	Date

Vaccination

Date	Vaccine	Date	Vaccine	Date	Vaccine

Registration

Date Due

Important Addresses

Name ....

Address ....

Phone ....

Name ....

Address ....

Phone ....

Name ....

Address ....

Phone ....

Name ....

Address ....

Phone ....

Judy Reinen has had a camera in her hands from an early age. Following in her father's footsteps, Judy started Creative Shotz Photography in Auckland, New Zealand, where she has built a reputation for unique wedding and portrait photography.

Judy loves animals and is passionate about photographing them. She owns a blue-point Persian cat called Yabba Dabba Doo, who "purrs so loudly his nickname is Tractor", an adventurous tortoise-shell Persian called Pancake and a Tibetan terrier named Basil.

"It has been such a pleasure to photograph each dog and cat. I'm constantly sidetracked. I want to cuddle them all. Each dog and cat has been a star and loved all the fuss. After my Great Dane, Major, passed away, I wished that I had a complete record of his life. I decided to make a series of Record Books so that everyone can have a lifetime of memories of their special friends."

Judy has won numerous international awards, including the prestigious Master of Photography title from the NZ Institute of Professional Photography.

Titles available in the *Animal Antics* series:
Cat Record Book
Dog Record Book
Cat Address & Telephone Book (two formats)
Dog Address & Telephone Book (two formats)

ISBN 1-57977-004-5

Concept and Contents © 1996 Creative Shotz Limited

ANIMAL ANTICS ™

Published in 1997 by Havoc Publishing Inc.
7868 Silverton Avenue, Suite A
San Diego, California, USA 92126

For further information on other Animal Antics products, please write to us.

Design by Trevor Newman
Printed through Bookbuilders, Hong Kong